The Courage to Wait:

The Courage to Wait:

A Memoir of God's Goodness and Faithfulness

Lea Javier-Giesbrecht

CITI OF BOOKS

Copyright © 2025 by Lea Giesbrecht

All rights reserved. No part of this publication may be reproduced, distributed, or transmitted in any form or by any means, including photocopying, recording, or other electronic or mechanical methods, without the prior written permission of the copyright owner and the publisher, except in the case of brief quotations embodied in critical reviews and certain other noncommercial uses permitted by copyright law. For permission requests,write to the publisher, addressed "Attention: Permissions Coordinator," at the address below.

CITIOFBOOKS, INC.
3736 Eubank NE Suite A1
Albuquerque, NM 87111-3579
www.citiofbooks.com
Hotline: 1 (877) 389-2759
Fax: 1 (505) 930-7244

Ordering Information:
Quantity sales. Special discounts are available on quantity purchases by corporations, associations, and others. For details, contact the publisher at the address above.

Printed in the United States of America.

ISBN-13:	Softcover	979-8-90124-405-0
	eBook	979-8-90124-406-7
	Hardback	979-8-90124-407-4

Library of Congress Control Number:

Our willingness to wait on God reveals the value we place on the object we're waiting for!
Excerpt from Dr. Charles Stanley

You can't lose being obedient to God.

The journey I'm sharing is about the Miracles of God in the lives of two individuals who have sought the will of God in their lives. This is a personal and inspiring testimony of faith, highlighting the belief that obedience to God, despite life's challenges, leads to unfailing provision and miracles. It emphasizes divine faithfulness, emotional and spiritual strength and the ultimate benevolence of a loving Gracious God.

This is the **story of Walter and Lea Giesbrecht:**

A Love story under Divine Orchestration

Walter Wiebe Giesbrecht, is the fifth of ten children born to Abram and Maria Giesbrecht, a German Mennonite family, Pioneers of Chaco, Paraguay. Walter grew up in a Christian home and was taught the importance of holding on to the Biblical values. His parents are loving and God-fearing Christians. His mom always prays every night by their bedside and always asks her children to know the Lord in a personal way. She was a very hard working and god fearing woman. Walter's father was a very hardworking and a devout Christian man and a great provider. Walter's parents were born during the pioneer days of The Mennonite migration in Chaco, Paraguay where, alongside with the first pioneers in Chaco. They both experienced the hardship and hard work of starting a livable place from bottom up. Walter also had experienced the struggles and life of a pioneer. He was the 2nd generation born of the pioneer days. In spite of the hardships and struggles, Abram and Maria Giesbrecht raised their family of 10 in faith, in hope and in the knowledge and relationship with God as the source of their strength. Walter's mom died from melanoma cancer at an early age in 1985. Walter's father died years later during the 2021 COVID pandemic.

Walter's faith in God resulted from the teaching and nurturing from his parents. He attended church activities growing up and became a Christian when he was just a teenager during a revival meeting held in Paraguay. He answered the call of the Lord by asking God to come into his heart and received the Lord Jesus Christ as his personal Savior and Lord. He walked with the Lord consistently as he could since then.

During one of the youth meetings, Like every teenager, Walter asked the Lord to reveal to him the special girl whom he would like to marry someday. He asked the Lord, specifically for a woman who is a Christian, loves the Lord and possibly from Asia *(he was impressed about people from Asia after studying the countries and the people)*

Walter only wanted God's will for a lifetime partner and pledged to God not to date anyone until the girl of his dreams will unfold under God's revelation. That, was his conviction.

As time passed (he was in his early 20's), he asked the Lord once again about the woman he was praying about but there was no answer from the Lord. Walter continued to wait upon God's time and continued working on his own 350 acre farm in Paraguay. He continues to be involved in his church in Neuhof Mennonite Church.

He loved serving the Lord even at a young age. His dream when he was young was to serve God and **wanted to work harder so that he can generously give to those in need, the needs of the church,**

pray for everyone and to visit the sick. (Little did he know that God was preparing him for a special task years later in a foreign land in Armourdale Baptist Church, Kansas City, Kansas for many years).

Years later, Walter has become a family man who works hard everyday to provide the needs of his family, church and to those in need. He has a serving heart and a generous spirit.

The Mennonite denomination has a non for profit entity called Mennonite Central Committee and in that organization has a specific program called, MCC- International Visitors Exchange Program. This program is designed to bring young people from all over the world to come to North America, to live, to learn the language and to build relationships among the people for an entire year. These young people will work and stay with host families in their stay in the USA or Canada.

The year of 1993, Walter applied to the youth Program of the Mennonite Central Committee. He hoped to be chosen to represent his church.

The process of being chosen to participate is a little bit slim because each Mennonite church in Paraguay usually has so many applicants. All applicants have to undergo an intense interview and thus, elimination occurs as well. So, the chances of being chosen were slim.

In spite of all that, Walter persevered and applied. To his surprise in that particular year, he was the only one who wished to participate in the program from his home church.

Therefore, he was chosen to go without sweat, I would say, that's a miracle from God in itself, paving the way to meet the love of his life that God designed. *He wrote:* "Six years ago, it was my wish to go to the United States. But, I really didn't think it would happen. During the seven months of waiting, I thought a lot about being a trainee. I knew everything *would be new and I couldn't speak English. I am a little scared but I am willing to go if chosen." Little did he know that obeying God paved the way for God's match making plan for a wonderful life with the love of his life designed by God only for him.*

It was through **the MCC International Visitor Program** held in the USA, where God's revelation of a perfect match which was designed by God to last forever is revealed.

Two people will soon meet. Let's start from the very beginning, in God's providential meeting, a very good start of a Love Story under God's loving design

Lea Patena Medrano Javier, the youngest of 12 children, was born to a Politician father and a stay at home mom, Felimon and Guadalupe Javier of Batangas, Philippines.

She grew up in a Christian home and was taught Biblical values to be lived by throughout her growing up years, which she adapted in raising her own family together with Walter. Lea has always loved the Lord ever since she was a young child. Just as her older sisters always say," Lea is always at the church doing whatever needs to be done even at a very young age". Her dream is to become a Missionary and to come to the United States of America.

As a young child, she loved to gather children from the squatters area and teach Bible stories and provide simple snacks for them. Teaching children about the Love of the Lord is her passion even when she was just a little girl as young as 9 yrs old.

Lea's mom died at a young age from an enlarged heart in 1985. Her dad died seven years later of a heart attack too.

Though Lea has been involved in the church growing up, she didn't become a Christian until the age 12 when a group of staff from Campus Crusade for Christ came to her home church and shared the Gospel. She was taught that to be saved is to confess her sins to the Lord and receive Jesus as her personal Savior and Lord. It was explained very well to her by the Campus Crusade Staff that going to church and being good is not enough to go to heaven and be saved when one person die. She thought a lot about it and felt a strong nudge in her heart to confess her sins to God and finally asked the Lord to forgive her sins and asked Jesus Christ to come into her life as her personal Lord and Savior and be in the throne of her life.

Her walk with the Lord has always been like a relationship with a very close best friend. She always talks to God in many different ways; talking to Him out loud but a lot of her conversation with the Lord is in writing. She writes to God about everything about her frustrations, her joys, complaints and anything that comes to her mind and her daily experiences about her daily existence. God has always been her best friend ! She cries to God and talks to Him when no one is around for her. Her insecurities, her lack of self

confidence is one of her struggles in life and the only one that she goes and confides her own emotion is to God. She feels so close to Him.

As a teenager, when all her friends were having relationships, it was hard for her not to question God about her own life, the questions lingered such as, " am I not beautiful enough to be noticed and to be loved ?" are questions were constant in her mind. While others are having boyfriends, she has none and it devastates her as all teenage girls do.

One conversation she had with God was about the pressure of having a relationship. For some odd reason, she always liked western/white people. She loves the color of their skin and their long beautiful pointed nose with a nice bridge. She tried meeting different Americans and Europeans by doing penpals but it didn't materialize.

One day, she asked the Lord and she wrote it in one of her journals saying, *"Lord, will you please give me a man that I will marry someday. Lord, our youth pastor told us that we should be specific when we ask you what kind of a person we want for a lifetime mate, so here it is, Lord."* Lea continued, *"I want a guy who is a Christian, a man who loves you and loves me and if possible has a white complexion like those Americans and has a long pointed nose. "*

Years passed in her 20's, she asked the Lord once again about the special person she was longing to have yet, still, there was no answer. She continued to wait upon the Lord in spite of the unanswered prayer.

Lea decided to focus in her studies and obtained her Bachelor's Degree in Theology from The United Church of Christ in the Philippines Pag-Asa School of Theology. She was one of the first graduates of the school. She was able to finish early because of her prior college education from Ateneo De Davao University where she had taken classes on Agriculture Business and Engineering.

After graduating from the Seminary, she served as one of the pastors of the main church in the City, The United Church of Christ in the Philippines, a church of 2,000 membership. While serving the church, she later was given a full scholarship for her Masters Degree in Religious Education and graduated from Ateneo de Davao Jesuit Seminary (St. Ignatius of Loyola)in Davao City, Philippines in 1995.

To graduate in the masters program in Theology under Catholic Jesuit school was very difficult for her because she has a Protestant belief and the only Protestant student. One of the struggles she experienced was when she did her thesis on the subject of the Church. She graduated with flying colors and had the most wonderful experiences she will never forget.

In Late Spring of 1993, Lea visited her sister's office in Manila. Brenda (Lea's sister) worked at the Mennonite Central Committee. While she was at the office of her sister, she saw an application to the program of the Mennonite Central Committee International Visitors Exchange Program. She picked up the papers and filled up the application then placed it back on the desk of the director. She flew back to her city, not realizing that her action would lead her to the fulfillment of her dreams *(to come to the USA)* and will receive God's answer to her question and prayers from God.

Few months after she left Manila, she received a phone call from the Director, The Country Representative of the Mennonite Central Committee Philippines, Mike and Becky Hoffkamp, asking her to meet with them in Manila. When she agreed, they provided her the ticket to fly to Manila for a quick interview and to apply for an entry visa to the USA at the US Embassy. She was told that they usually have many applicants to participate in this program but for some odd reason, the office were so busy and ran out of time to advertise and interview people. Therefore, since Lea was the only applicant, and they already knew her, they decided to choose her to represent the Philippines for this program.

Lea flew to Manila. Becky Hofkamp and her, went to the US Embassy to get J-1 entry visa with no sweat. Lea was not interviewed by the consul instead they just automatically gave her a multiple entry visa to the US. **This is another miracle of God!** It was obvious that God is in control, *(note that the process of getting an entry visa to the US is very difficult wherein, first, one has to stand literally in a mile long line just to get an interview and usually you are not guaranteed of a visa, most likely denied after the interview* **but in Leas' case, it was Divine Intervention! Another miracle of God)**

The beginning of a perfect love under God's loving Direction soon will take place

Life as an International Visitor Exchange Program (Trainees)

Walter (German Paraguay) and Lea (Philippines) were among the 78 young people from 27 countries arrived to participate in the Mennonite Central Committee International Visitor Exchange Program (IVEP). A one year program in which 78 young people from 27 counties, with very little or no English came and lives in the USA for a year. This program is designed to bridge the gap between countries and to share each other's culture and for the participants to learn English. They all arrived in Akron, Pennsylvania in July 1993 for a 5 day orientation and received their first assignment for the year.

It was an awesome sight, people talks to each other in different languages like the story of The Tower of Babel in the Bible. Lea was chosen to be the choir director of the IVEP choir (all participants are called an IVEP) They had 3 concerts within a year; Bloominglen, Pennsylvania during the orientation: Fairview, Oklahoma during the midyear 5 day conference; and Akron, Pennsylvania during the last 5 day year-end conference.

Walter was assigned for a year to a farm in Aurora, Nebraska with his host parents Ron and Lois Preheim since Walter is a farmer back home in Paraguay. Lea was assigned to the Chicago Mennonite Learning Center (a K-8th grade private school) located in the South Side of Chicago by Midway Airport where she taught Bible and Music and in the Summer, she spent 2 months as a Pastor interns in Colorado Springs, Pueblo, and Manitou Springs, Colorado. She hiked up to the Summit and down Pikes Peak in Colorado Springs, Colorado. *(**Lea was on the front page of Black Forest Community paper for hiking Pikes Peak in the summer of 1994**).*

Lea's first experience living with a host family was in Pennsylvania with the Detweillers'. They were very nice people. Her first culture shock in the USA was as she expressed herself saying, "*how come there were no people walking around*" **(Lea was used to seeing people as soon as you walk out of your front door). Another culture shock was** the use of a shower. After a long flight from the Philippines, she needed a shower. She tried to take a shower but the shower was different than what she is accustomed to. She was so embarrassed to ask, so she suffered taking a shower kneeling down since she didn't know how to operate the shower. She didn't know how to get the water to come out of the shower head. Few days later, she found out that it was easy. All you have to do is, to lift the small lever on the wall to make the water come out of the shower head!

Walter was one of 10 people from Paraguay. They spoke mostly German. He had it all together but the language. After the Orientation, everybody left for their assignment. Lea stayed behind in Pennsylvania because the school year had not yet started in Chicago.

Lea Patena Javier in Chicago

After the Orientation, Lea and SibuSisiwe from Africa were on their way to their assignment for a year and took the Greyhound bus bound to Chicago, not knowing of the many challenges she was about to face!

Upon arrival, SibuSisiwe from Africa was greeted by her host family but Lea was told that her host family backed out of hosting a trainee (to host Lea). She arrived in the Windy City of Chicago, new in the country, new in the city and no friends and family and no host parents to welcome her. **It was unbelievably shocking and hard for Lea. (how in the world they had forgotten to mention this to her before her departure) She** was very disappointed and scared but, she was a fighter. This is what her father, a well travelled and well-educated man taught her; to always be strong and be positive in the midst of problems and difficulties. Her father instilled in her mind Proverbs 3:5-6 and that God is in control.

"Trust in the Lord with all Thine Heart and Lean not on your own understanding. Look to Him in all of your ways and He will direct your path"

Soon enough, she met the principal of the school, **Ross and Marge Liechty** (also new at the school and who didn't know anything about this program). They were kind enough to accommodate her in what Lea needs. She was placed at the **Volunteer Service single house** located in 4733 S. Lamon St.Chicago, IL (it is located in the south side of Chicago by Midway airport). **She moved into the house alone.**

One day, she asked the Principal to give her a lot of tokens and a map of Chicago and the bus and train routes. She was given lots of tokens!

One Saturday morning, after breakfast, she bravely took her tokens and map and took the buses and trains and spent the whole day familiarizing the transportation system in Chicago. At the end of the day, she was able to accomplish her goal of knowing the City and how to get around using the public transportation.

Her friend the Rev. Dr. Bill Osborne stopped by to see her on his way to Pennsylvania and his visit was a great relief and excitement for her. She told him *"is this what you call the United States of America? I am ready to go home!I don't like it here!"* Lea was lonely and she felt so alone and bored in a big City of unknown (to her). Then, Rev. Bill told her that there is a nice lady whom he wants her to meet and she lives in Chicago. **It gave Lea hope.**

After Bill left, the lady whom he was talking about, called Lea. That night, she came and picked her up and took Lea for dinner *(Leas' first restaurant dinner in the USA, Olive Garden (walters favorite today).*

Elizabeth Roser is a very kind and wonderful lady and a great friend since they met and in the years to come. She lived in Arlington Heights which is north of Chicago while Lea lived in the "hood" in the south side of Chicago.. Elizabeth was brave enough to drive down to Midway just to meet Lea. What a great person!! **Lea can't thank God enough for His love and provision!** She needed a friend so bad and God provided her one through **Elizabeth Roser.**

Lea, also has experienced being chased 3 different times while living in Chicago. The first time, she was chased by 4 white males in their white car. They yelled at her in a slur voice (she believed they were high with drugs) saying *"hey, lady!!!* **What are you doing ?"** and they got out of their car and started chasing her on foot. Lea ran as fast as she could without looking back and all she heard was profanity. Lea was petrified with fear when she arrived in her house. She cried so hard out of fear! She was alone, scared and no one to cry on and to embrace and console her.

A few weeks after, another scary thing happened. Two men followed her on foot but then, instead of being scared, she turned around and faced them and asked them, **"what do you want?** " putting her brave face forward. For some odd reason or another the two men turned around and left as if they have seen a ghost, could that be an angel beside or behind her that made them run ? Lea's thoughts later **". God's protection, indeed and God's angel was with her)**

> A few months later, a white van followed Lea for some distance. The white van followed her slowly in the street of Cicero, Chicago. Whenever she turned, he was there. She was so scared. She saw a McDonalds and ran in there and waited *(but the man in the white van waited too)* until the white van left. Soon enough, Lea saw the man drive off and she ran back home and was scared.

The struggles and dangers she faced, made her stronger and her faith in God grew stronger and her dependency in God was vital in her existence while in the big City of Chicago especially living in the south side,

Later, after living in Chicago for 10 months, she was so proud to say "I love Chicago!"

When the school year was over, Lea became an intern Pastor in Black Forest Community Church, Manitou Springs, Pueblo, Colorado and she was one of the Counselors in the church Camp. Overall she said it was a great year as a Trainee in The United States of America!

Walter Wiebe Giesbrecht in Aurora, Nebraska

Walter Wiebe Giesbrecht arrived at the farm and residence of Ron and Lois Preheim. Unlike Lea's challenging experience, Walter had it made from the beginning. He was

welcome wholeheartedly and lovingly by his host parents. Walter worked in the farm and learned a great deal from Ron Preheim about operating different heavy machinery. He did very well and he impressed his host father of how quickly he learned. He was a natural farmer indeed.

Walter experienced something new and a scary one as well.

One day while he was driving the tractor a tornado was passing Aurora, Nebraska. He didn't think much about it since he never experience being in a tornado, so he just kept on driving. His host father had been calling him but the communication was down. He saw the corn bin gone the next day. *(actually he was about 50 to 100 yards away from the corn bin. The wind was very strong and he was still on the tractor just before it was blown away)* What was he thinking of not taking cover!! But again, *he never experienced tornado and so, he didn't think much about it and continued to finish his work. He was safe !*

The Courage to Wait

The Preheim was very generous and loving to Walter. He was given a car to drive around and was given money for gas and spending money for his vacation to Grand Canyon. *(Lea has to find her own transportation and money for her vacation)*. He also enjoyed the cooking and the care of Lois Preheim. She always made sure that a can of peaches was available because that was Walter's favorite. He was well taken care of by The Preheim then and even later when he got married.

Ron and Lois were so impressed by Walter's intelligence, peaceful demeanor, great sense of responsibility and good work ethics. It was proven when they went on vacation one day but forgot to tell Walter that a load of cattle will arrive that night. Sure enough, the load came and Walter took the responsibility of unloading and did what needed to be done. Walter did it very well.

Walter was a great Trainee and responsible. He did something that Ron and Lois appreciated and made a comment to him *"I have never had a Trainee who could handle it all by himself and knew what to do and didn't need to be told what to do. He cares about everything and everybody..."* Ron was beaming with pride with what Walter did.

There were other Trainees around where Walter was; Abram Harder, Rie Iwase and 2 more trainees. They usually got together and had fun on weekends. They also went on vacation together. Ron and Lois Preheim provided Walter everything he needed. When he went on vacation to see the Grand Canyon (he took the helicopter to see the whole scenery of Grand Canyon) and California, Ron made sure that the car had as full tank gas and gave Walter spending money. They spoiled Walter to the max. He had a great time living with The Preheims!. What a great couple and their love and generosity extended when Walter got married and to the present.

Walter was so grateful for his assignment. He wrote:" *There are many things I like about being in the US. I enjoy my work and life in*

Nebraska. Singing in the church choir was very good. Something new I learned from Ron Preheim, my sponsor and host. I learned how to irrigate corn and how to feed cattle. The snow was very special for me too. I enjoyed the snow but not the cold weather".

IVEP Mid Year & Year-end Conference

After 6 months, all the trainees met once again and this time, everybody could speak English and had a lot of fun being reunited again. They became one big family. They hugged and genuinely expressed how much they missed each other.

It was during the mid year conference in Fairview, Oklahoma that Walter and Lea met for the first time.

Since Lea was the choir director, every trainee knew who she was but Lea didn't know everybody. Their conference was held in Fairview Mennonite Church. (Rev. Charles Priddy was the pastor the year before Walter and Lea became trainees. He was also the same pastor who later called and offered Lea a job in Armourdale Baptist Church 15 years later)

After the cultural and choir concert, Walter, Lea and, Liz Hunsberger *(The Director of the program)* were watching Abram Harder (one of the trainees who play the harp) packing his harp. Liz asked Walter, **"do you know how to play the harp?"** and Walters response was **"no, but I sure know how to play Lea!"**.
Liz laughed so hard and we all did!

After the mid-year conference everybody went to their new assignment for another 6 months. Walter continued to stay with The Preheim. The director gave Lea an option to stay or to change after hearing Lea's challenges in Chicago but Lea chose to stay there.

All Trainees gathered together once again for the last time in July of 1994. It was called, The Year-end conference held in Akron, Pennsylvania.

Few days before all 78 young people had to go back home, The Mennonite Central Committee loaded all of them in several buses and took them to see Washington DC and allowed them to stay for a whole day visiting the White House, Lincoln Memorial and to many great places to see.

It was during the end of the one year program, 5 days before all the participants had to go back to their own country that Walter and Lea finally spent the day together.

One day, Walter happened to be sitting between 2 Asian ladies, Rie Iwase from Japan and Lea Javier from the Philippines. Lea asked Walter what would he be doing when he get back home? And Walter's response was, **"I want to be married to either one of you"** Rie said" *No"* but, Lea said ***"yes, why not!"*** in a jokingly manner. (Lea was so outgoing and liked to joke around) She did not think that this would be the beginning of a lifetime with Walter which God had intended. The truth is, God was slowly making His plan known and revealing to them the answer to both of their prayers.

At the end of July of 1994, the program ended, and all participants went home to their respective countries, including Walter and Lea.

A month later, Lea received a long distance phone call, (an expensive one as well…$5.00 /minute) from Paraguay!
An Expensive call from Walter, Pursuing Lea!
What a brave man, I say….

In the course of their monthly phone calls, Walter asked Lea if she would be willing to visit his country when he came to visit her the following year. And as usual, Lea said *"yes"* and even aske*d "Are you going to bring the ring?"* Walter's response was *"Yes"* Walter didn't know what size of ring to get for Lea but he purchased anyway in Paraguay hoping that it would fit her and it did! **(Another Miracle of God!)**

Walter purchased 2 round trip tickets from Paraguay to the Philippines. The tickets cost **$2,000.00/ person.** Also, Walter remodeled his house in preparation for Lea's visit.

Would Lea stay in Chaco, Paraguay? Would Walter be happy in the Philippines? Would they both be happy in their marriage and would it last a long time? Forever? A marriage of two different cultures, ethnicity and social customs, would it work?
These are the questions and doubts of many people as Walter and Lea were planning Life's greatest relationship ordained by God…
The Gift of Marriage!

The Roller Coaster of Life
(The honeymoon is over and the facts of life are taking over)
Written by Lea

Life is the best gift the Lord has given to mankind in which man should acknowledge and be grateful for this wonderful gift each day. When you wake up in the morning, see the sun shine and realize that you are alive and God has given you another day to live, you need to be grateful to our Lord God Almighty!

However, Life cannot be called a wonderful life apart from ups and downs of life which includes many disappointments, discouragements, trials failure and frustrations.

Everyone needs to remember that even though, you know the Lord, you are not exempt from experiencing these things. We all get angry and frustrated with our lives.

All things in the world changes; people, society etc. One moment you are up and the next moment you are down. Once you lived a single life, next thing you know you are married!

Marriage is a very good example of change. Marriage in itself is hard but most specially a marriage that is so culturally diverse, so international and has a great language barrier! In this kind of marriage, it needs a lot of time, patience, understanding and more love for each other with many forgiveness and more love and commitment. For, it will be tested in different ways and if this marriage is not grounded with Love, Commitment and most specially if not grounded with God, it will definitely fail!

Marriage will be tested by different changes that life brings. The solidarity of love for each is revealed. Two things will happen: One, You get bitter and remorseful, and then throw in the towel and call it quits or Two You try to understand and be a better spouse to each other and pray and hope for a brighter marriage and relationship. These choices need to be chosen as you live a life as husband and wife. Strong Faith in God is essential for any marriage to thrive. God is the source of everything.

THE MARRIAGE PREPARATION:

Lea and Walter had their courtship and relationship via long distance. Then, on **June 1, 1995,** Walter flew in to the island of the Philippines crossing 2 major oceans, the Atlantic and Pacific, flying almost 42 hours, from Paraguay, to Brazil, to Miami, to San Francisco, to Korea, to Manila and then to Davao, Philippines. It is indeed a journey of a lifetime ... to pursue the Love of his life amidst the distance half around the world and the vast expense for a young man of 27 yrs old with little English just to pursue what he thought was God's special person for his life.

He also experienced major jet lag because the Philippines is 14 hours ahead of Paraguay, a big time difference. Geographically, Paraguay and the Philippines are 18 degrees longitude from one side to the other. Walter's English then was not as fluent as it was later. He flew in to the other side of the globe (literally) to marry the girl of his dreams, conquering oceans, jetlag, and discouragements from family and relatives! Was it worth it?

You need continue to read ....

Walter arrived at Ninoy International Airport in Manila with no one to greet him. Lea's sister Brenda who lived in Manila waited for him 12 hours prior to his arrival. Lea forgot to mention to both of them about the time difference. Walter managed to secure a hotel and asked the manager of the hotel to purchase him a ticket to fly to Davao *(an hour and a half flight more)* where Lea was.

Walter arrived in Davao the next day and was greeted by Lea, Marisa (Lea's sister) and Gil (Lea's oldest brother). Upon Walter's arrival, Lea was busy with work, was translating books from English to Tagalog for a Muslim Ministry, Preaching at the Christian Radio Station, Pastoring a church and a language tutor for Korean and American Missionaries. She had no time for Walter on that day that he was turned over to Marisa to be his companion and guide for the day until evening.

At dinner time, Walter was surrounded at the round table by all of Lea's brothers, sisters and in-laws. Lea's brother asked him, **"So, Walter, what is your plan?"** Walter blushed! He was speechless but kept his peaceful demeanor. Lea saved him by saying, **" Hey, guys, leave him alone. We have not even had the chance to talk about anything." Whew!!! What a relief for Walter!!!**

Later that night, when Walter and Lea were alone, he showed Lea the wedding ring he had purchased for her. It fit perfectly right!

Another of God's miracles!

Walter didn't actually propose to Lea. It was more like Lea asked Walter prior to his arrival. Walter's thought was, if Lea would not marry him, he will just consider it a great vacation for him. He was so patient and understanding with Lea.

However, Lea was undecided whether to accept Walter's proposal as she had many other opportunities namely: 1 She already had accepted the position as Associate Pastor in a greater Manila UCC Church where the former President of the Philippines went, 2 She was offered a full scholarship to finish her doctorate 3.She was given a job offer to be the Manager of the Christian Radio Station 4. Here came Walter who travelled many hours and was now proposing a Marriage for a lifetime! **Lea was in whirlwind!**

Her challenge was which one to choose since all of these were good for her future!

In her confusion, she sought advice and wisdom from God and from her friends from the Radio Station FEBC (Far Eastern Broadcasting Corp). After a series of consultations, she finally told Walter yes. And since Walter could not stay for more than 30 days in the Philippines with a tourist visa, they needed to plan to be married within 2 weeks,

June 24th, 1995 came the wedding. Was it an easy procedure and preparation? A big NO was the answer!

Walter and Lea had no idea that it would be so difficult and complicated to contract marriage with a foreigner. When they went to get their license, they were told that Walter needed a document from his embassy stating that he is eligible to contract marriage in the Philippines. He obviously didn't bring it with him so, he needed to get it from his embassy. But, the problem was, his nearest embassy is in Japan!

But, after so much red tape and politicizing in the City Hall of Davao City, Philippines, they received their license without Walter going to Japan. The wedding was planned within 2 weeks. So, Lea talked to everyone, family members, relatives and friends and church people. Everyone enjoyed the preparation and everyone contributed to everything; from the very tiniest details of the wedding preparation to the largest. The reception was a potlock at the residence of Lea's sister Marisa. The purchase of Lea's wedding dress was sponsored by the Korean Missionary and the dress was done within 1 and a half weeks. Walter's Filipino Barong Tagalog was purchased at Aldivinco. The beautiful wedding cake was donated by Lea's sister in law Viola Javier and the honeymoon was sponsored by Lea's cousin, the owner of a hotel in the city! The church people contributed their talents, time and whatever preparations were needed in the church. All of Leas 17 nieces and nephews were in the wedding entourage. All of Lea's brothers and sisters prepared the food, entertainment and more.

It was a great preparation! We call it in Tagalog "Bayanihan"(working together) God continue to be at work in their lives!

THE WEDDING OF A LIFETIME
The fulfillment of God's Promise to Walter and Lea
June 24, 1995, 10AM
United Church of Christ in the Philippines
Davao City, Philippines
Rev. Pal Dumanig, Officiating

The day before the wedding, it rained so hard that Lea was so worried since the reception was to be outside. She was so stressed out, and as always talked to the Lord about her frustrations regarding this mater. The Lord was so patient with her and just listened to her complaints. The day of the wedding, the rain stopped and it was a beautiful day for a wedding. God sent rain the night before to cool the weather for a perfect wedding.

Isn't God so wonderful and very gracious, loving and patient? *God knows Lea's wits and character and He allowed Lea to vent like a spoiled brat child to her Father while Walter as always was calm and peaceful. The wedding was not elaborate nor fancy but*

the ambiance and the atmosphere were so pleasant and at ease and everyone was so happy and joyful! And the reception was wonderful and you could not have asked for a more beautiful wedding.

When the reception was over, Walter and Lea helped in cleaning up before they went to their hotel for their honeymoon. The next day, they went to The Suemith Farm together with Lea's brothers and sisters and families and relatives and enjoyed eating, swimming and eating exotic fresh fruit from the farm. It was a very delightful and fun day to celebrate a new beginning with family! Lea's uncle and his wife, Teodoro and Santa Patena were present as well.

Walter and Lea became One on June 24, 1995.

"Marriage does not depend on feeling alone but a Commitment to Love, Honor, Respect and Support each other, No matter what Life brings."

Walter and Lea made the commitment before God in the presence of many witnesses on this day *(they didn't realize on that day that their marriage will be tested in hard and mighty ways and would almost be blown away had it not been for God's loving hand holding them and embracing them in their Lifetime Commitment as God ordained it to be.)*

The Journey begin

Walter and Lea was separated for 6 weeks, 2 weeks after they got married. Here's the reason why they were separated soon after they got married. Walter and Lea were at the airport to leave the country, to go to Paraguay, Walter's home. However, Lea was not allowed to depart because she had no entry visa into Paraguay and Philippines will not allow her to leave the country.

Walter left the Philippines. Started the 42 hr flight back home, yes, married but no wife to show for upon his arrival to Paraguay. Perhaps, he regrets going to the Philippines and got married but the truth is, he never waver his faith in God and he firmly believed that Lea is the woman God has planned for him and so, he waited patiently with God's assurance given to him. He just waited until Lea can join him in Paraguay

    Problem begins about Immigration for Walter and Lea

To acquire a visa for Paraguay, Lea first need to go to Japan but before she can go to Japan, she has to be interviewed by the Japanese consul to determine that she will be given an entry visa Lea needs to be interviewed by the Consul of Japan. The nearest Paraguayan Embassy is in Japan. If granted a Japan visa she had to fly to Japan to be interviewed by the Paraguayan Embassy Consul to get an entry visa for Paraguay. **It was a very complicated procedure and an expensive one as well.**

Truth be told, if you live in a third world country, acquiring an entry visa to any country is not guaranteed. It's a risk, and this risk is something that Lea is willing to take.

In spite of frustrations in front of Lea's eyes, she trusted the Lord. Indeed, the result was great because
God maneuvered everything!
He is in Control! How did He do that ?
Let's keep on reading :

It was a long process beginning with communicating with the Consul General of Paraguay via phone and finally, the Consul General waived

their regulations and procedures in obtaining a visa. The Consul general of paraguay told Lea that this had never been an option to waive a personal interview prior to granting a visa.
However, he consented that Lea would just mail her passport to the Embassy. After receiving Lea's passport by mail, they stamped the passport for an entry visa to Paraguay and sent them back to her.
Lea didn't need to fly to Japan nor apply a visa to enter Japan!
-**Another of God's Miracle!!!**

Walter and Lea were reunited and lived at Walter's farm in Chaco, Paraguay in September, 1995. Would it be a Happily ever after ? Far from it

Just like newlyweds, struggles were evident. Their lives were far from being happy. It was not the kind of life in which both were happy, Walter was for a portion of it but Lea wasn't. They forgot to share each others' social differences prior to getting married.
Walter grew up on a farm all his life and Lea grew up in a really big City (atleast one Million people). Walter was used to livestock while Lea had never been so up close with the cows let alone touch them!

Walter was a dairy farmer and had his own 350 acre farm. On one occasion, as Walter left in the morning to be in the field, he asked Lea to let the calves in first followed by opening the big fence for all the mother cows to drink water. Walter asked Lea to separate the moms and their babies in preparation for milking!
Was he out of his mind!!! Was Lea's thought.

Later that afternoon, Lea did what Walter asked him to do. She opened the gate to let the calves in, and then, the other gate for the mother cows. Guess what Lea did? As soon as she opened both gates, she ran as fast as she could and jumped over the fence!!!! She was terrified! She didn't know that 3 neighbor children, ages 2,6 and 8 were laughing so hard watching Lea run like crazy.

It was indeed a great entertainment for them!

Also, Lea had to do the daily house chores such as: cooking, baking, and cleaning of which Lea was not use doing it. Back in the Philippines, she had a maid to cook, clean and bake for her and even make her bed everyday! But, Lea tried her very best to be a good and domesticated wife like all of the Mennonite wives in Chaco!

On another occasion, Lea baked bread but it was as hard as a rock outside but soft inside. *"This was her first time to bake."* Then, an Indian beggar came to the house and asked for bread. Sure enough, Lea gave them the bread she baked. Little did she know that the beggar would go to the neighbors and told them that *"the lady from far away gave them this bread!"* Was Lea embarrassed? Are you kidding? Of course! But, she took it lightly when she heard about it and said to herself, *"Never will I bake again!"*

Living on the farm was very difficult for Lea. She missed being surrounded by people and speaking her language and English for that matter.

In December, 1995, Ron and Lois came and visited Walter and Lea in their residence in Neuhof. She was thrilled and very excited. She spent a great deal visiting with Lois while Walter spent time with Ron. Lea savored and enjoyed every minute spent with them because in her thought, these will soon be gone since they are only visiting for a week Also, Lea didn't know German and everybody only spoke German, so the visit of Ron and Lois Preheim was heaven sent.

Lea tried her very best to adjust to the lifestyle in the farm. She was able to speak and understand the high German. **However, as hard a she tried farm life and to be a domestic farm wife, it didn't work well and the truth really shows that this was not Lea's cup of Tea!**

Problem come one after another. One of which was, **Immigration**. Lea cannot get her immigration paperwork straightened out and also living in a colony, in the farm miles away from the city was extremely difficult and very stressful. These added to Lea's unhappiness and loneliness.

Also, three times, Walter faced a near death experience. He was driving the tractor while making a waterhole. Then, all of a sudden his tractor slowly slipped down into the hole. His brother saw it and ran to his rescue and pulled his tractor out with his. On another occasion, he was about to milk the cow very early in the morning and the mother cow bucked him so hard that he was underneath the humongous cow and she kept on bucking

him with her horns. He was saved by his dog Shaeper. The dog jumped on the cow which gave Walter a chance to crawl out and escape. He was saved by a good dog! All these happened when Lea was still asleep. Then, the last incident was Walter was working in the field when he was attacked by hundreds of bees and got stung all over his face and body. He jumped in the pond and was saved. He came home and told Lea what happened. Lea was terrified of the life in the farm and these added to her unhappiness!

So, out of Walter's great love and concern for Lea's well being and happiness, he unselfishly decided to sell all the cattle and everything else except the farm to move and live in the Philippines hoping to have a happy marriage en route to the USA. (Poor Walter!!)

During this time, Lea's great missionary friends by the name of Rev. Bill and Donna Osborne, were living in Wellington, Missouri. He was the Pastor of a church called St Luke's Evangelical Church.

They left Chaco, Paraguay in March, 1996.

On the way to the Philippines, they decided to stop in the USA since they had an entry visa to the USA. Walter and Lea introduced themselves to their own friends as husband and wife. Lea was introduced to Walter's host parents Ron and Lois Preheim and Walter was introduced to Lea's friends, Foster and Elizabeth Roser and Rev. Bill & Donna Osborne. They both stayed in Wellington, MO and met great people from Saint Luke's Evangelical Church for three months.

Because Walter was German, he was greatly welcomed in the church and in the community and Lea was accepted too. There, they met great friends who later became their long time friends and supporters: Larry and Pauline Tilly, Wayne and Joyce Tilly, Neal and Linda Niendick, Sharon Piepmeir and more.

Both of them hoped to stay for good in the US however circumstances didn't allow them to stay(not in God's time yet). They had no working permit, only a visitor visa, besides Lea found out that she was pregnant. Donna took her to the doctor and later that night, The Osbornes' and the Giesbrechts' celebrated Lea's first pregnancy.

But, Lea's pregnancy was very dangerous and it was very expensive to stay in the US, so, they decided to continue on their journey to the Philippines,to live and to deliver their first born baby **(Nieko William Javier Giesbrecht)** and continued to wait for God's leading on where to settle.

As hard as their circumstances, Walter and Lea continued to wait upon the Lord.
God is still in control of their lives!
They lived in the Philippines for about 10 months.

Life in Davao City, Philippines

While in the Philippines, they kept their communication open with St Luke's Evangelical Church. However, living in the Philippines didn't make both of them happy either.
Lea was but Walter was not

Walter has never stayed in a big city in his life let alone to live there. When the baby was about to be born, he was so unhappy and kept his struggles and problems to himself.

When Lea had some contractions, she was admitted to the hospital to deliver the baby. While in the hospital, he wanted to be with Lea during the delivery but the nurses did not allow Walter to be at the delivery room. He waited patiently for 30 hours outside the delivery room! He was so frustrated and could not believe that all of Lea's family were in the private room in the hospital waiting joyfully for the arrival of the baby. He was so unhappy with the presence of so many people everywhere. He just then covered his face with a blanket to release his emotion because he didn't want them to see his frustrated feelings.

Later, when Lea found out how Walter felt at the hospital, she felt so bad. Lea forgot to tell Walter about the Philippine culture that when someone is sick or when a baby is to be born, families will be at the hospital to give support and show their love for them. It was not meant to hurt him. Both of them forgot to discuss the difference of each culture.
Western culture and Filipino culture are quite different. Walter was not happy that he was not the first one to announce the arrival of the baby. ***This was one of the cultural differences Lea and Walter forgot to discuss.***

When Nieko William Javier Giesbrecht was born, everybody was so excited to see and the first thing they asked was, **"What kind of a nose does the baby has? Is it like Walter or Lea's?"**. **A nice pointed nose like Walter is always admired in the Philippines!**

Nieko William Javier Giesbrecht was made in Chaco, Paraguay, Processed in the USA and Delivered in Davao, Philippines via caeserean by Dr. Laya Freires and Dr. Leyla V. Rivera (Lea's best friend) on December 30, 1996 at 5:00 PM

Lea and Walter continued to live as a family with their young son in Davao City. Lea went back teaching at the Seminary, translating books from English to Tagalog, part time pastoring a church and helped missionaries learn the Filipino language.

A couple of Missionary friends and their god-parents who stood up on their wedding day, were a great help and support to both for Walter and Lea but most specially to Walter;

The Rev. Fred and Rev. Barb Adams and The Rev. Mike and Sharyl Langford!

Lea was very happy living in the Philippines where all her friends, families, jobs and church were, but Walter was not happy. The only person that made him happy and helped him go through daily living was his son Nieko, whom he took care of day and night. **The two of them were inseparable!** Walter changed diapers more than Lea. **Nieko was his life, his security and his happiness!**

Walter and Lea experienced many hardships and trials in their marriage; culture differences, outlook in life, adjustments in their relationship and Immigration.

Walter had problems in getting his Immigration straightened out in the Philippines. Walter and Lea had to fly to Manila to do all the paper work and it was a tedious and expensive process as well.

These trials and difficulties and pressures were taking a toll in their marriage. Walter also was not happy just being a stay at home dad

In one incident, while at home, Walter and Lea had a big fight about everything.
They were so mad at each other that they passed notes to each other, Lea in one room and Walter in the other.

Later, while Walter was playing with Nieko on the floor, Lea tried to take Nieko from him but Walter wouldn't let go of Nieko. Nieko (a baby then) was in between and literally being pulled back and forth by his mom and dad! **Ridiculous, isn't it?** But, it did happen. Their rage towards each other and their problems had built up and were on their verge of throwing in the towel and **call it quits!**

But, God is still in control. God is not finished with His plan for them yet! *(Like the process of making a beautiful vase, the clay needs to go through a lot of molding, unmolding, then being placed in the oven with a very, very hot temperature and then the finished product is beautifully made and revealed).*

When both of them had calmed down and reflected and focused on their marriage and problems, they both agreed to start fresh and made up. They both prayed and thanked the Lord for their trials and victories and for their marriage. It took them great courage and humility to swallow each one's pride to say,
"I am sorry and please forgive me". It only became possible through the grace of God and not by their own doing. Both of them want to follow the will of God. They ended the night by making a Covenant of Commitment entitled:

"Each for Each Other and Together for God"

"Today, we, Walter and Lea have made a commitment and a covenant in the presence of our Lord God Almighty, that we will try our very best to understand more, to love more and to have plenty of room for patience and to support one another from now and until the end. And that no matter

what life may bring to us, we will love and support one another under the wings and guidance and strength of our God, our Lord and Savior. And May these four verses of the scriptures remain in our hearts and believed it more seriously and May these be a constant reminder of our Covenant and our walk with God in this marriage now and forever!

"I will put you in the cleft of the rock and cover you with my hand" (Genesis 33:22)

"Guide us clearly along the way you want us to travel(in this marriage), so that we will understand you and walk acceptably before you". The Lord says, " My presence shall go with you and I will give you rest" (Genesis 33:12-13

"For I know the Plans I have for you, declares the Lord. Plans to prosper you and not to harm you. Plans to give you hope and a future."
(Jeremiah 29:11)

"That we will make this covenant of marriage successful to the fullest in serving God;" Each for each other and Together for God"
Signed under God's presence that we will abide everything that was written, so help us God"

During these time, when Walter and Lea's marriage was in turmoil and they later made up, The Mission committee of St Luke's Evangelical Church in Wellington, MO, spearheaded by Sharon Piepmeier, suggested to the Church committee that they sponsor Lea and Walter Giesbrecht to come back to the US.

The plan is, Lea will be working with Pastor Bill Osborne as an Associate Pastor, doing the Christian Education of the church.

St Luke's Evangelical Church sent an invitation letter to sponsor The Giesbrechts'. (Another of God's Miracle).

They received the letter and submitted them to the US Embassy for an entry visa. They were approved without the need of an in person interview. (another of God's miracle because the US Embassy usually never grant anybody an entry visa without an in person interview).

They now had a visa to come to the USA.
The church provided them with plane tickets but not spending money. It was hard to leave the country and travel without money. Lea swallowed her pride and wrote to her friend Elizabeth Roser who lived in Chicago. She told her about the situation and out of her generosity, she sent Walter and Lea $200.00 to take with them on their way to the USA.

The Giesbrechts' in The United States of America

May 5,1998, The Giesbrechts' arrived in the USA after 24 hour flight. They were picked up by Rev. Dr. Bill Osborne at Kansas City, Missouri International Airport. Pastor Bill stopped at WalMart and bought car seat for Nieko, who was one year old. The toddler fought against sitting on the car seat because he has never sat in a car seat before, he always sits on somebody's lap while travelling. Finally, they arrived in Wellington, Missouri and were greeted by Linda Niendick, Pauline Tilly Donna Osborne, Anne and Drew. It was a very happy reunion.

The insurmountable problems began engulfing them upon arrival. They were told that the church can't hire Lea as full time. This was a big problem, since the application to the Immigration and Naturalization Service stated that Lea need to have a full time job with a full time and substantial salary in order to be approved to work by the INS.

God touched everybods lives to help the Giesbrecht's'. First, they met Dr. and Mrs. Gordon Clark who offered them to live in their basement.

Later, Lea was asked to teach at a Christian School at the church school of Rev. Pete Winstead. But, Lea needed a fulltime job so working at the church school didn't work because it closed the door shortly after Lea started teaching.

Pastor Bill Osborne tried to help Lea find a job and he knew about the Bridges of Hope program down in Armourdale, Kansas City, KS and mentioned Lea to the board and scheduled a meeting.

They went to the Armourdale Area and met with Pastor Gary at the Methodist Church who was one of the members of the board. Afterward, they had a tour of Armourdale and while there, they casually met The Rev. Charles W. Priddy at the Community Center (**he used to Pastor the Church in Fairview Mennonite Church in Oklahoma a year before Lea and Walter were a trainee and had their mid-year Conference at that particular church**).

Weeks later, Lea received a phone call from Rev. Chuck Priddy who wanted to know if Lea will be interested in working at Armourdale Baptist Church doing children and youth work on a trial basis.

Pastor Chuck quoted this verse:

"For this reason, since the day we heard about you, we have not stop praying for you and asking God to fill you with the knowledge of His will through all spiritual wisdom and understanding. And we pray this in order that you may live a life worthy of the Lord and may please him in every way; bearing fruit in every good work, growing in the knowledge of God, being strengthened with all power according to his glorious might so that you may have great endurance and patience and joyfully giving thanks to the Father, who has qualified you to share in the inheritance of the saints in the kingdom of light. Colossians 1:9-12

(This verse was God's answer to their problem of needing a job to fulfill the INS requirement of a full time job.)

Lea answered the call after a car load of people from Armourdale Baptist Church came, namely Pastor Chuck and Wanda Priddy, Barry and Elizabeth Bradley, and Richard McGuffin, to interview Lea and Walter.

On September 6 1998, Lea received a welcome letter from the church clerk, Marie Burris (who later became the greatest adopted mom for Lea) stating the official call of the church.

The Giesbrechts' can now begin the process of Immigration to legalize their status so that they would be legal to work. With the help of Rev. Bill Osborne, the letter from Armourdale Baptist Church, St Luke's Evangelical Church,and Saint Luke's Hospice **(Lea was also recommended to work at Saint Luke's hospice. The director of the hospice also signed to help in the immigration process of the Giesbrecht)** were ready for submission.

Walter and Lea's lawyer submitted a letter to the INS stating that Lea had a full time job, splitting time among three entities, Armourdale Baptist Church, St. Luke's Evangelical Church and Saint Luke's Hospice of Kansas City, Missouri (Pauline Tilly, a friend and at the same time the secretary of the church, sent all the necessary papers to the immigration lawyer, Atty. Roger McCrummen, an Immigration Lawyer Walter and Lea hired to help with their papers.

The lawyer told Walter and Lea that he had never had any case like this before and they were only given a 50% chance of hope that their visa will be approved. The lawyer didn't sound positive. But, Walter and Lea embraced God's leading and security that they were not so worried but continued to live under God's directions.

**GOD is still in Control!
Never underestimate the Power of God,**

In **January of 1999**, they received a phone call from **Pauline Tilly, the secretary** of the church and told them that they were approved to work in both churches and at Saint Luke's Hospice by the Immigration and Natural Service. They were given **a non Immigrant Religious Visa for 5 years** and then after 5 years, they are eligible to apply for an **Immigrant working visa** which was granted for another 4 years. Then, when the time passed, they were eligible to apply for US Citizenship. (fee are paid each filing and lawyers fee as well which cost the Giesbrecht thousands of dollars)

While waiting for each step of pursuing US Citizenship, Walter and Lea and Nieko continued to live a life under God's guidance.

With discipline and hard work, they became financially stable. When they came to the US, they only had $200.00 in their pocket, the money given to them by their friend Elizabeth Roser.

Seven years later because of God's goodness and great provision and help, the Giesbrecht became financially stable. They bought their first house in Shawnee (the story of finding this house was also God-send and leading and a miracle in itself), vehicles paid in full and were able to travel internationally once a year.

God's miracles was only possible because God touched the lives of so many people, as they extended their financial, moral and spiritual support to the Giesbrecht. It started with The Osborne, who adopted them and literally supplied their needs especially during their first three months in the USA. The generous offer of Dr. and Mrs. Gordon Clark to live with them in their house free of rent literally helped the Giesbrecht in all of their other needs. Nieko was a sickly child and having no insurance was difficult for them.

Once again, God's provision was evident as God brought The Clarks in their lives to help them with their needs using their Medical expertise. They loved the Lord and loved The Giesbrecht as well.

Another major problem the Giesbrecht experienced was when Lea became very ill and having no medical insurance was not a joke. Once again, God brought people to help her. The group of ladies in Armourdale Baptist Church heard about Lea's condition and was moved to help her. Karla Higgins, Lea's friend and a member of the Streeter/Colas/Gillman's Circle, suggested that the church give Lea $2,000.00 and it was approved. The Council also decided to have a special offering for a month to help them. It was a great blessing for The Giesbrecht. God is great! Lea's condition stabilize and became normal.

In the course of waiting for their Immigration, Lea became pregnant again for the second time.

On January 10, 2001, Walter, Lea and little Nieko stopped at Truman Medical Center in Kansas City, Missouri for Lea's weekly check up. They casually scheduled seeing the doctor on the same day of the church business meeting.

Upon arrival at the hospital for the check up, Lea didn't realize that she was actually in labor and that the baby was ready to come out and see the world. There was no sign of labor pain unlike the first one. It was also a very easy pregnancy.

Walter and Lea were not ready because it was still early for her due date and so, they did not have anything with them when they came to the hospital. They were living in Odessa Missouri at that time, one hour away from Kansas City, Missouri.

Walter was told by Dr. Gordon Clark to go and take the 4 year old Nieko somewhere and returned to the hospital as quickly as he can because the baby will come out soon.

While Walter took Nieko somewhere, Dr. Gordon Clark did all the admittance paper work for Lea. (Another Great blessing!)
The Giesbrecht had no health insurance but Dr. Clark helped Lea in everything and made it all easy for the Giesbrecht.

Nieko was handed to Bud and Marie Burris who gladly accepted him without complain and took on the responsibility.of watching him while Walter went back to the hospital. Walter and Lea can't thank them enough for their kindness.

Walter then returned to the hospital and for the first time, actually experienced being there for the birth of their son. Around 5 PM, Dr. Clark said, *"Here he comes Walter!"* and pulled the healthy baby, cut the cord and placed him on Lea's arms. They were beaming with pride. Gathel Bryan Javier Giesbrecht was born and what a beautiful healthy baby.

Later that evening, Gathel & Lois Bunch and Karla Higgins (Lea's best friend) came and Pastor Chuck Priddy came as well. They were the first visitors of Lea and the newborn baby, **Gathel Bryan Javier Giesbrecht, the first USA citizen from the family of Giesbrecht.** Walter, Lea and Nieko have to go through the process of Immigration but not Gathel !

The Sept.11 tragedy made Immigration tougher and The Giesbrecht were also affected. It prolonged their wait to apply for Citizenship. But, The Giesbrecht held on to God's leading and promises. It was **not easy but Faith in God made them endure trials and difficulties with flying colors.**

Their attitude in all these things was, their lives are not theirs but God and because God leads them along, He will make things possible beyond the impossibility from human perspective. They had experienced over and over again in their lives the wonder of God's power and leading especially about Immigration. It was very hard to believe if you don't see the end but the Giesbrecht took a leap of faith and believed that the Living God is faithful to them.

On June 30, 2002, Lea was **Ordained in the Ministry by the American Baptist Church Denomination.** She presented her paper in front of 50 people with lots of questions and passed with a comment from The President of The Central Baptist Theological Seminary,
"I have no question for you but a commendation for a well written paper"

The Armourdale Baptist Church helped Lea and Walter in everything. The church and members prayed fervently, and lovingly petitioned to God for the fulfillment of their dream of becoming a US Citizen.

Then, on December 27, 2009, Walter and Lea finally were eligible to apply for US Citizenship and applied without the aid of a lawyer (it cost them $1,800.00 fee for Immigration and Naturalization). They did the paperwork on their own with the help of a friend **Elizabeth** in proofreading and making sure everything was filled out correctly.
They didn't anticipate the speed of the process because within weeks of filing they were scheduled for finger prints and the big US Constitution and By-Laws oral and written test. **Walter and Lea took the test separately and Walter did great with no sweat. Lea on the other hand did well and passed.**

Then, April 30, 2010, Walter and Lea were sworn in at the courthouse of Kansas City, Kansas at 12:00 noon.

Walter, Lea Giesbrecht and Nieko are full pledged USA citizens. **Gathel Bryan Giesbrecht (their youngest son) is a US Citizen by birth.**

It was a very heart- warming and memorable ceremony. Pastor Bill Osborne, Bud and Marie Burris, Elizabeth Roser *(she flew in from Chicago just to attend the Ceremony)*, Gathel and Lois Bunch, Nancy Huddleston, Bob and Donna Kissinger, Len and Priscilla Skinner, Tracy Clark, Carol Graney, Linda and Neal Niendick, Larry and Pauline Tilly were the people who came to witness the Ceremony! **It was a great Celebration!** Elizabeth Roser who was from Chicago said that the Ceremony was great unlike the way they do in Chicago.

When the Giesbrecht came home from the ceremony, they saw their house and yard decorated by Tracy Clark, congratulating them for their wonderful achievement!

The following day, May 1, 2010, The Giesbrecht family was given a wonderful **US Citizenship Celebration by their loving Church Family in Armourdale Baptist Church spearheaded by Nancy Huddleston and her committee.** Friends from far away came to greet The Giesbrecht and to celebrate with them.

God is in Control and in His time His plan will be revealed and He DID!

The process of getting legal document to work and eventually receive US Citizenship is not easy. It was tedious, nerve wracking, costing thousands of dollars but most of all Prayers, Patience and Rest on God's Will to be Done are vital because **He is in Control!**

God held Walter and Lea in His hand and they allowed His will to be done in their lives **"Be strong and courageous. Do not be terrified. Do not be discouraged. For the Lord your God will be with you wherever you go." Joshua 1:9**

Praise the Lord!

The stability of our lives and the situations we face daily, is solely dependent on God and God alone if you want your lives to be of great success!

On Memorial day of 2010, Mr. James Bundy Jenkins, a very distinguished man of Armourdale of Kansas City, KS was so proud of the Giesbrecht that he told the Channel 9 Newsmen that **The Giesbrecht** just became US Citizens. **Channel 9 went and interviewed them and it was aired that night! What a blessing from God for their great accomplishment!!**

Walter and Lea have experienced the loving and gracious hand of God and His provisions in all aspects of their lives. It was difficult, expensive and long, yet, they made it by the Power and Leading of God in Jesus Christ!!...

The story of Walter and Lea Giesbrecht is a story of Miracle after Miracle. This is the story of God's providence in the lives of two separate individuals with different ethnic backgrounds and lifestyles. But, in the midst of the many differences they have one thing in common and that is, **they both believe and love the Lord Jesus Christ as their personal Savior and Lord and as The King and Ruler of their lives.**

This is a Living Testimony of the Giesbrecht as they mentioned : "**Our stability of our lives on earth, our journey and success is grounded in and only in our Lord Jesus Christ.**" They received God's gift of Salvation. "*They accept it, and then, lived a life of Thanksgiving and ThanksLiving*" *(excerpt from* God's word made plain by Mrs. Paul Friederichsen).

God scatters His miracles, minor and major. Sometimes we encounter them without recognizing them as miracles. "Do not be afraid of their threats, nor be troubled. The Lord of hosts, Him you shall follow; LetHim be your fear."

Update:
27 years later (2025), they continue to walk with the Lord and has now enjoyed watching their adult children one just got married, the other one is engaged. They both grew up to be wonderful Christian young men.

Through the years, Walter and Lea have achieved many things that people said they will never get and accomplished ... indeed people who were saying this were right because Walter and Lea would never have been able to achieve them if they relied on themselves but they relied on the Power of God. They have faith and obeyed The Almighty ! Because of these, Walter and Lea experienced the Miracle of God one after the other in their lives.

Walter and Lea had been married for 30 years (2025) going on 31.

To God be the glory Great Things He has done !

ACKNOWLEDGEMENT:

Many years in the making and Walter and Lea would like to express their heartfelt gratefulness to all that God touched to be an agent of His love to The Giesbrecht:

To Our Living Almighty God, in Jesus Christ and The Holy Spirit
To the Bible, Gods Word who is our anchor and daily Guide
Rev.Dr. Charles Stanley and his messages who give us support daily
Walter Giesbrecht for giving up his farm and everything for Lea
Saint Luke's Evangelical Church for the sponsorship
The Mission Committee, Especially Sharon Piepmeier, Chairperson
Rev. Dr. Bill and Donna Osborne (for supporting and loving us)
The Armourdale Baptist Church
Tracy Clark, Carol Eisenbraun and Saint Luke's Hospice
Rev. Chuck and Wanda Priddy (for believing in us)
Larry and Pauline Tilly (our faithful and forever friends)
The Tilly Farm (for giving Walter an opportunity to work at their farm)
Elizabeth Roser (Lea's forever supporter and friend)
Rev. Joe and Judy Garza (for all the prayers and support)
Dr. and Mrs. Gordon Clark (for hosting us and helping us in many ways)
Ron and Lois Preheim (for their loving support and generosity.
They
loaned us a Buick Park Avenue for an entire year with insurance and all.
The Streeter/Gillman circle for helping Lea when she was very ill.
Bud and Marie Burris for being our "Dad and Mom" which means a lot to us. Nancy Huddleston, Bob and Donna Kissinger, Gathel

and Lois Bunch, Len & Priscilla Skinner, Karla Higgins and to all not mentioned who sacrificially have given their time, money, and effort to make this thanksgiving event a great one.and for all your love and support Elizabeth Jenkins for proofreading this writing and for being my great best friend and prayer supporter.

Diana Weatherman- my dearest best friend who helped us in many ways.

To God be the Glory Great Things He Has done. Blessing to you all.

<u>For I know the Plan I have for you declares the Lord. Plan to Prosper you and not to harm you. Plan to give you hope and a future Jeremiah 29:11</u>

Walter, Lea, Nieko, Gathel and Buddy Giesbrecht

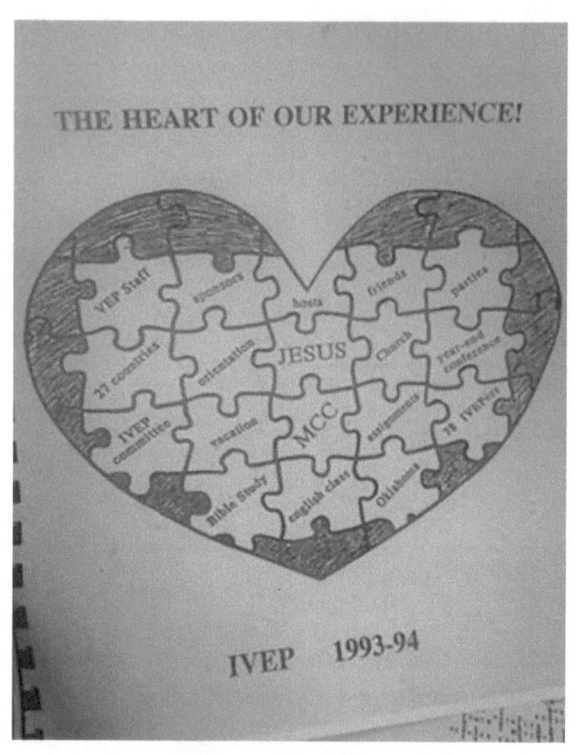

78 young people from 27 countries came to participated in International Visitors Program Mennonite Central Committee

IVEP Days

<u>Walter and Lea's first and only date</u>

Walter as a single young man

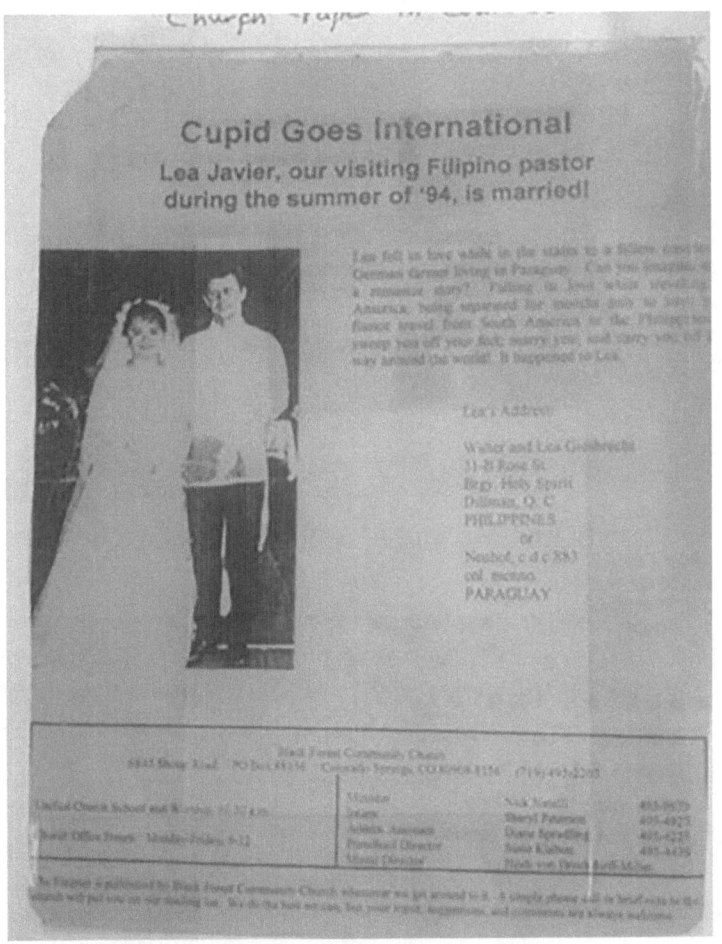

Cupid Goes International. Lea fell in love while in the United States to a fellow traveler German living in Paraguay. Can you imagine such a romantic story? Falling in love while travelling in America, being separated for months only to have your fiancé travel from South America to the Philippines to sweep off your feet, marry you, and carry you off half way around the world! It happened to Lea! Colorado Church Newsletter

Newly wed Mr. and Mrs. Walter Giesbrecht

Lea's brothers and sisters on Walter and Lea's wedding day

The Adams Family

The Langfords Family

Bill and Donna Osborne

Lea Milking the Cow and Walter at their farm in Neuhof, Chaco, Paraguay

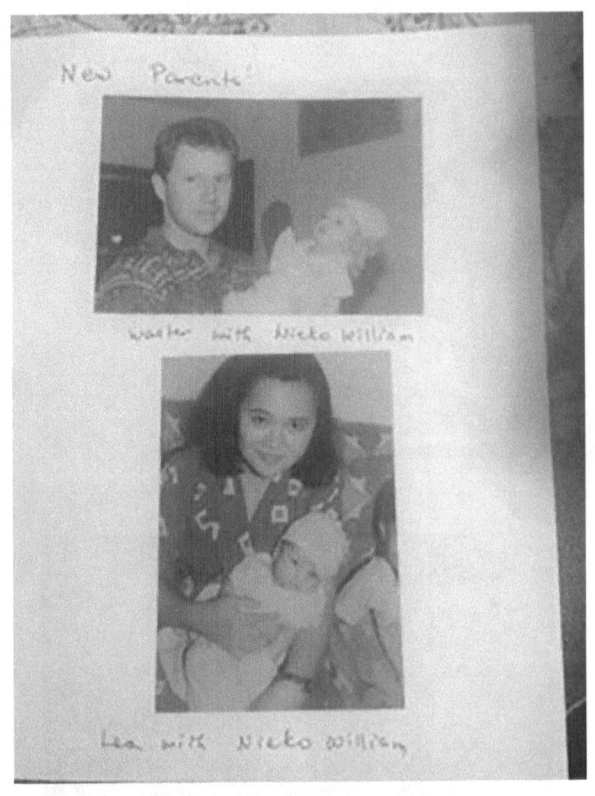

Nieko William Javier Giesbrecht 12/30/96

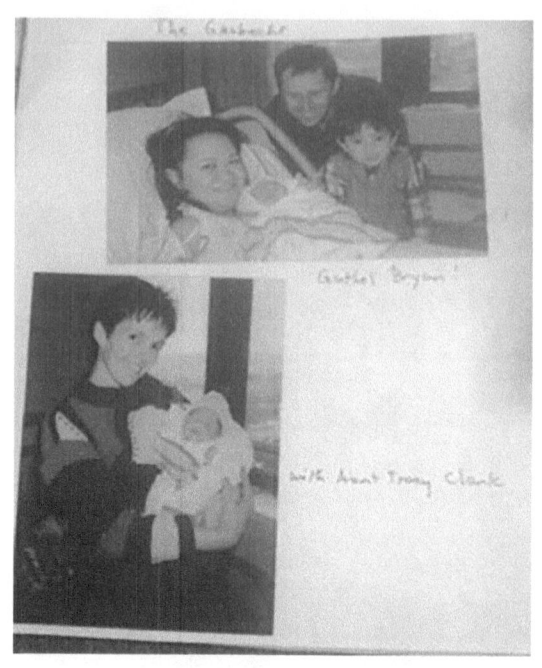

Gathel Bryan Javier Giesbrecht 01/10/01 with Dr. Gordon and Tracy Clark

OFFICIATING JUDGES

U.S. Citizenship Oath Taking!

<u>Tracy Clark and Lea</u>

Marie and Elizabeth

Gathel and Lois Bunch

The Jenkins Family

US Citizen Day, April 30, 2010

<u>At the Courthouse with The Tilly's and Elizabeth</u>

Bud and Marie Burris Lea's adopted mom and dad

My adopted mom Marie Burri

John and Sharon Piepmeier

Bob and Donna Kissinger

Len & Pricilla Skinner and Nancy

Foster and Elizabeth Roser with Walter and Lea

Our Loving Parents:
Abram and Maria Wiebe Giesbrecht and Felimon and Guadalupe Patena Javier

My Loving Adopted Parents:Bud and Marie Burris

www.ingramcontent.com/pod-product-compliance
Lightning Source LLC
LaVergne TN
LVHW041103060526
837225LV00010B/3